The Lost Dog

Edited by Edwin Way Teale

THE INSECT WORLD OF J. HENRI FABRE

GREEN TREASURY

THE WILDERNESS WORLD OF JOHN MUIR

THOREAU'S WALDEN

Other Books by Edwin Way Teale

ILLUSTRATED BY PAUL LANTZ

The Lost Dog

BY EDWIN WAY TEALE

DODD, MEAD & COMPANY

New York

Library of Congress Catalog Card Number: 61-12054
Printed in the United States of America

Dedicated to
GERALD WEAR
with admiration for his
lonely, enduring search for
PONCHO

Introduction

Near the end of my 20,000-mile journey gathering material for *Autumn Across America*, I found myself early one morning on a forest road twenty miles south of the Columbia River, in western Oregon. Heavy frost silvered the shed roofs in clearings all along the way. As the sun rose higher and the frost melted, mist curled upward from each building so it seemed on fire, smoldering in the chill autumn air. It was under such circumstances that I reached the village of Alder Creek and came to Rose Moody's Tavern, a weathered roadside restaurant set in an opening in the woods.

Inside, a counter with wooden stools formed a square-angled horseshoe that occupied the center of the single large room. A few booths were ranged along one wall and, beside a jukebox in a corner, a large frame, holding newspaper clippings and pictures of a man and a dog, leaned against the wall. This was the setting in which I encountered one of the few authentic heroes I have ever met.

He is the man in the photographs. His name is Gerald Wear, pronounced to rhyme with deer. The dog in the pictures is his dark German shepherd, Poncho. The story of their adventure in the wilderness of the Wallowa Mountains is one I told first in a chapter of the *Autumn* book and here repeat in somewhat expanded form.

When this account of a lost dog and a man's indomitable search first unfolded piece by piece, that day beside the forest road, it seemed to me that I was following some true-life allegory, with a lone man pitted against the giants that all mankind encounters—the giants of exhaustion and frustration and loneliness and despair. More handicapped than most, Gerald Wear met them all. The peculiar circumstances of his enduring search, the handicaps that narrowed his chances of success, the remote and uninhabited land where the quest was centered, the pressure of time running out—all these enhance the poignancy and drama of this story of a dog that was lost and a man who refused to abandon him.

The Lost Dog

One October day, a man and his dog went hunting. The man was Gerald Wear. The dog was Poncho. For nearly ten years they had been daily companions, living together at the village of Alder Creek, not far from the foot of Mount Hood, in western Oregon.

Yet Wear had never heard his dog bark, for the man had been born completely deaf. Poncho had never heard his master speak, for Wear also had been born dumb.

These two, the man who could not speak or hear and the dark German shepherd dog that was always at his side, often went to the woods together. They followed

The land of the Wallowa Mountains, which they were penetrating, is one of the most rugged and remote areas remaining in the United States. If you look at a road map of Oregon, you will see that the far northeastern corner of the state is largely blank. It contains only a few far-scattered communities. No major road penetrates the fastness of its jumbled peaks, knife-edged ridges and high plateaus. So sharp are some of the ridges that it is impossible even to ride a horse along their tops.

Ten of these Wallowa peaks rise above nine thousand feet and almost as many more lift their tops above eight thousand feet. Bordering this highland wilderness on the east is Hell's Canyon, the Grand Canyon of the Snake River. It is one of the deepest gashes on the face of the earth. For forty miles, here, the green-tinted water races and tumbles over the bottom of a chasm that has an average depth of more than five thousand feet.

In remote valleys, far back among the Wallowa Mountains, a few ranchers live. Beside these, forest rangers and hunters are almost the only visitors to the area. So wild is this region that even today no detailed maps of the country have ever been made. Only primitive, wheel-track roads thread the interior. This was the forbidding, almost uninhabited land into which Wear and Poncho rode that day.

All that morning they rode upstream beside the rush-
ing Columbia River. They made time over the smooth
highway, for rough traveling lay ahead. In the afternoon,
they left the river behind and struck out across rolling
land. Then they were among forests and mountains.
Dusk fell. In darkness, they climbed higher into wilder
and wilder country.

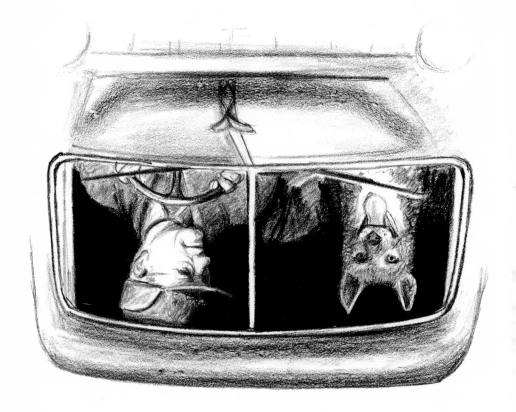

mountain streams on fishing expeditions. They roamed
in the forest and over high meadows among the peaks,
hunting for big game.

On this October morning, dawn was just breaking
when Wear climbed behind the wheel of his light truck.
Poncho scrambled to the seat beside him. Hunting gear
and camping equipment crammed the enclosed body of
the red machine. Wear slammed shut the doors and
started the motor. Together they headed east to hunt for
elk in the wilderness of the Wallowa Mountains, nearly
three hundred miles away.

It was after nine o'clock that night when they reached Billings Meadow, a high plateau set among the mountains. Wear pulled to a stop and climbed down. Poncho leaped after him. In a few minutes, the man was busy putting up the tent, building a campfire and preparing a belated supper. Poncho, after a day spent in confinement and inactivity, dashed about in the darkness. Tireless as a wolf, able to run long distances, he coursed this way and that. He raced along animal trails, led on by innumerable scents in the night.

When the smell of frying meat joined with that of the campfire smoke, Wear looked around for Poncho. He was unable to find him. He sat by the fire, eating his meal alone, expecting to see his dog come racing in out of the darkness each minute. When he finished his meal, Poncho was still gone. For an hour or more Wear piled wood on the fire, sending the flames shooting high in the night to provide a beacon for the dog. When at last he went to bed, Poncho still was missing. Several times during the night Wear awoke and piled more wood on the fire, hoping the flames would guide the wanderer back.

The thermometer was falling and there was the smell of snow in the air. Toward morning a few flakes drifted down. Soon they were swirling past the campfire. In an hour or so the flurry was over. But it left behind a thin white blanket that covered the land, obliterating whatever trail Poncho had left behind. Wear now had no way of tracking him. Somewhere in the immensity of jumbled peaks and broken valleys, he knew, his dog was alone and lost.

What had happened? Had he raced away after some coyote? Had he kept on and on, hot on the scent of some game animal? Had the turning and twisting pursuit of a jack rabbit left him confused in unfamiliar territory? What occurred during his first hour on Billings Meadow nobody knows. To this day, Wear has no clew as to how Poncho became lost. All he knows is: He never came back.

In the cold dawn of the next morning, the man cooked

and ate a hasty breakfast. Then he set out on what was to be the first of many days of searching. America's greatest dog hunt had begun. For fourteen hours Wear hurried this way and that, seeking, but never finding, some sign of his lost dog. He clambered up ridges and ascended the skirts of the surrounding mountains to scan the country below. Noon came and passed. Without stopping for lunch, he hastened on. Dusk had fallen when he stumbled back into camp. Nowhere had he seen a moving thing that resembled Poncho.

In a few minutes, the man was busy, putting up the tent, building a campfire and preparing a belated supper. Poncho, after a day spent in confinement and inactivity, dashed about in the darkness . . . tireless as a wolf.

Too tired and worried to eat, Wear crawled into his
blankets only to rise time after time during this second
night in order to keep the campfire roaring on the
thousand-to-one chance that, wherever he was, Poncho
might see the flames or might catch the drifting scent of
the wood smoke.

Once more, at daybreak, Wear was on the trail. All
that day and the next and the next he searched. And
each night he kept the beacon of his campfire burning.

He had combed the whole of the wild, remote Billings-
Meadow area before he admitted defeat. Poncho, he
knew, had gone beyond the vicinity. He was wandering
somewhere, no one knew where, in the vast Wallowa
wilderness.

This western high country is a land of long winters.
The first killing frost, on the average, arrives before the
second week in September. On late-October nights the

thermometer may drop close to zero. The menace of early blizzards is always present. Unless he could find Poncho before snow and ice and cold locked in the mountains for the winter, Wear knew well, his dog would never be able to survive.

But even more than this consideration, another urged Wear onward in his frenzied search. This was the knowledge that Poncho, being a German shepherd dog, would be mistaken at first glance in the wild for a coyote. Every rancher's and every hunter's gun would be against him.

29

It was on the night of October 24 that Poncho disappeared. That was a Tuesday. At daybreak on the fourth day, Wear broke camp. Hastily piling his gear into the back of the truck, after a few hours of exhausted sleep, he headed south toward the nearest city, Enterprise. His first thought was to let as many people as possible know that his dog was lost and wandering among the mountains. In spite of his great handicap, his inability to talk to people, his inability to hear their questions, he set about eliciting help.

Writing out the facts again and again on a pad of paper, he visited highway officials who might see Poncho. They notified workmen on all the roads leading toward the wilderness. He got in touch with the state police. He visited the government men in charge of the Wallowa National Forest. He pleaded with everyone to tell all hunters going into the area that his dog was lost and not to shoot it. He obtained the help of the local newspaper, the *Wallowa County Chieftain*. In issue after issue, in the days and weeks that followed, it carried front-page stories on the progress of his lone-handed, seemingly hopeless hunt for his lost dog.

This done, Wear raced back to Alder Creek. He drew out all the money he had in his savings account. He stocked his truck with provisions. He put a cot and blankets in the back where he could sleep during the cold nights without putting up a tent. He purchased a new

compass. With almost all the money he had in the world
and with all the maps of the area that he could find—the
best being the one of the Wallowa National Forest put
out by the Forest Service of the United States Depart-
ment of Agriculture—he returned once more to the hunt.

What happened in the weeks that followed, I learned
from Wear himself when, one autumn day a few years
later, I visited him at Alder Creek. We sat at the counter
of the weathered roadside restaurant where he works.

34

This restaurant seemed to comprise almost the whole of Alder Creek. A square-jawed, pleasant-faced man with a shy smile, Wear was in his early forties. He fished from his pocket a peach-colored pad of paper and the stub of

a yellow pencil. Scribbling questions and answers on this pad, we conversed through writing and I learned the story, firsthand, of his long quest on the wandering trail followed by Poncho.

Poncho, Wear knew, was shy of strangers. No matter how lonely he might get, no matter how hungry he might get, he was not likely to go to a ranch or a hunter's camp for help. It was not that he was antagonistic but rather

that by nature he was reserved. He was a one-man dog. And as events amply proved, Wear was a one-dog man.

November came. Wherever a track led to an isolated ranch, Wear followed it to inquire about his dog. By the middle of the month, almost everyone in Wallowa County was looking for Poncho.

"What was the weather like?" I wrote.

"All the time snow. Two to six inches of snow. Temperature between twenty degrees above zero and two degrees below zero."

By sleeping in the rear of his light truck wherever
night overtook him, he was protected from wind and
snow. But not from cold. He slept with his clothes on,
piling blankets on top of himself in an effort to keep

40

warm. Whenever he dozed at night he dreamed of Poncho. Day after day he drove himself in this race with the
winter, in his struggle to find the lost dog before cold
and hunger ended his life. He was confident that, until

41

the snow became too deep and the cold too intense, Poncho would be able to survive by overtaking and catching small game.

Losing weight, sleeping fitfully, going often to bed supperless, Gerald Wear continued his roving search. Twice he came close to a nervous breakdown from exhaustion.

"Too much worry. Too little rest," he wrote on the pad.

But reports began to trickle in. A rancher here, a

hunter there, had sighted Poncho. But none could get near him. The first report came in from Cold Spring, in the far northeastern corner of the state, only ten miles from the Washington line and hardly six from the great chasm of Hell's Canyon and the boundary of Idaho. Wear raced north. For days he roamed over this lonely land, with the thermometer hovering close to zero, seeking some sign, some trail of Poncho. But he was too late. The dog had moved on.

Next a party of hunters reported that they had seen him in the wild country around Buckhorn Spring, some twenty miles to the south. Wear hurried in that direction. Once more he roamed on foot over a vast area, day after day searching from dawn to night. Here, too, the thermometer remained close to zero all the time. And in the dark at the end of each day Wear returned to the cold truck discouraged and alone.

"But I wouldn't give up," he wrote on the peach-colored pad.

As each report came in, Wear marked the spot where the dog had been sighted with a penciled cross on his general map of the area. He disappeared in the back of the restaurant and returned with the map in his hand. It was creased and worn. Its surface was smudged. Still visible were half a dozen widely scattered crosses. The third of these crosses represented a report that came in from a rancher near Zumwalt, twenty miles south of Buckhorn Spring. Once more Wear searched day after day and once more he met with failure.

Hunters next glimpsed the dog near an abandoned campfire in the wilderness country west of Zumwalt. Then he was seen near Tope Creek, thirty miles away and still farther west. The next report came in from Mud Creek, to the north. His erratic wanderings were carrying Poncho in a great hundred-mile, clockwise circle back toward the spot where he had first become lost.

Out of his movements a pattern began to emerge. Although Poncho was skirting ranches and avoiding hunters and strangers, he was going to the remains of campfires in search of his master. As days became weeks,

Wear, in mounting desperation, tracked down every report, every rumor. By now he had tramped hundreds of miles among the mountains. Each new lead he received came out of the remote interior days after the dog had been sighted. Always by the time he had rushed to the area the trail had grown cold. Although he is unable to utter a word, Wear can produce a thin, shrill, piercing call that Poncho knew. From the top of each elevation, he repeated this cry over and over again. But never once in all these weeks of his lonely quest did he catch a glimpse of the dog he sought.

WASHINGTON
OREGON

Mud Creek

⑦

⑥

Tope Creek

⑤

Wallowa River

1. *Poncho is lost here.*
2. *He is first reported here.*
3. *Hunters spot him here.*
4. *Rancher sights him here.*
5. *He is reported seen here.*
6. *Rancher glimpses him here.*
7. *Poncho is found here.*

Enterprise

Wallowa Lak

In his desperation, Wear now turned to the air. He
rented a light plane, piloted by an Enterprise aviator,
and searched for Poncho from the sky. Circling over open
meadows, following the valleys, climbing above the
ridges, skimming low over every stretch of likely country, the craft carried him in a wandering, zigzagging
course across the wilderness. For 375 miles, this aerial
search for the lost dog continued. Every second he was

In his desperation, Wear now turned to the air. He rented a light plane and searched for Poncho from the sky—circling over open meadows, following valleys, climbing above the ridges, skimming low over the wilderness.

in the sky, Wear peered intently down, scanning the ground for a small, dark shape he sought. But nowhere did his eye catch a glimpse of Poncho. He landed again at Enterprise at the lowest point of his despair.

Thanksgiving Day came and went. Wear, his endurance almost gone, spent the holiday in heavy-hearted search. A whole month now had passed since Poncho disappeared in the darkness of Billings Meadow. Time had almost run out. It was only a matter of days before the northern high-country winter closed in. Then search would be impossible. The lost dog would be overwhelmed by drifts and cold.

It was in the final week of November when word came from a rancher that only the day before he had seen Poncho in broken country some twenty-five miles east of Mud Creek. But he had not been able to get near him. This was the hottest tip of all and Wear dashed north, bumping and bouncing along the frozen ruts of a primitive road. This, he was well aware, was almost his last chance. Almost all his money was gone. His strength was nearly exhausted. In his lone-handed hunt he had walked more than 450 miles, had flown 375, had traveled a total of 1,752 miles, more than the equivalent of a journey halfway across the North-American continent. And every step and every mile and every day had been marked a failure. This was the situation at dawn on Sunday, November 26.

All that morning Wear hunted and called. It was near-
ing mid-afternoon when he climbed to the top of the
highest elevation he could find. There he could survey
all the surrounding country. Nothing moved below him.
His voice was nearly gone but he kept giving his shrill
cry in the forlorn hope that Poncho might catch it somewhere in the country spread out below him.

He had called for nearly two hours and was almost
ready to turn away when his eyes caught the movement
of a small black speck a mile or so away on the snow.
Wear redoubled his calling. Yes, he was sure. The speck
was moving slowly toward him. Its progress was almost
imperceptible. Three times it disappeared entirely, twice
descending into gullies and once being swallowed up in
a stretch of woodland. But little by little, stopping and
inching ahead, so weak from hunger and cold and fatigue
that it took nearly two hours to cover the mile, Poncho
kept coming.

Afraid he might lose sight of him, Wear remained where he was, uttering his thin, shrill cry at frequent intervals. Only when Poncho appeared in the last opening did Wear run down the slope to meet him. It was twenty minutes after four when he threw his arms around him. America's greatest dog hunt was over. Poncho was found at last.

For a long time he lay on the ground completely exhausted. Wear sat beside him. At first Poncho's ears were drooping. He seemed afraid of being scolded for disappearing. Then he revived. He ate some of the food that Wear had carried so long for this moment which he had almost, but never quite, despaired of seeing. Then these two together—the one-man dog and the one-dog man—descended the slope to the red truck that carried them home.

"Where is Poncho now?" I wrote on the pad and slid it along the counter to Wear.

He led me outside. As soon as we opened the door of the restaurant a dark German shepherd, sleek and strong, magnificently alive, came bounding across the road and over the frosty ground. Now nearly twelve, a little gray around the muzzle, Poncho was solid and healthy, all signs of his long ordeal gone. He sniffed me briefly and let me scratch his ear. But his interest in strangers was scant. As soon as I was done he nuzzled close to Wear.

He was his friend—the finest friend a dog ever had.

Edwin Way Teale is a literary naturalist who is described by *The Saturday Review* as a writer, naturalist and photographer who "excels in all three branches of his art." He has been awarded the John Burroughs Medal for distinguished nature writing. His books have been published in England and in French, German, Italian, Swedish, Finnish and Braille editions. He is a past-president of the New York Entomological Society, a member of The Explorers Club, Fellow of the New York Academy of Sciences and an Associate of the Royal Photographic Society. In *North With the Spring* he explored a new field, the natural history of a season. The story of a 17,000-mile journey, keeping pace with the advance of spring up the North American map, it forms the first of a projected series of four books on The American Seasons. *Autumn Across America* adds another volume to this monumental series. In an adventurous, wandering, 20,000-mile journey, it carries the reader from Cape Cod to California through the most colorful season of the year. Now *Journey Into Summer* takes the reader from northern New England along the shore of the Great Lakes, south through the corn country and into the high Rocky Mountains, for another 19,000 miles of nature exploration through the American summer. His books have an ageless appeal.

Paul Lantz, a fine portrait painter, has illustrated several outstanding books, including Walter D. Edmonds's Newbery Award Winner, *The Matchlock Gun.* He was brought up in the West, so is ideally suited to combine with Edwin Way Teale in enhancing a fine story with beautiful pictures, which he has done most successfully for *The Lost Dog.*